Hi Kim,

You are my lovely me
all the best in your next
see each other again in life.

From Van Ark
Bangor June 2016.
xxx

THE SPIRIT OF

SNOWDONIA

JERRY RAWSON

HALSGROVE

First published in Great Britain in 2007

British Library Cataloguing-in-Publication Data
A CIP record for this title is available from the British Library

ISBN 978 1 84114 666 9

HALSGROVE
Halsgrove House
Ryelands Farm Industrial Estate
Bagley Green, Wellington
Somerset TA21 9PZ
Tel: 01823 653777
Fax: 01823 216796
email: sales@halsgrove.com
website: www.halsgrove.com

Printed and bound by D'Auria Industrie Grafiche Spa, Italy

Introduction

The Snowdonia National Park – Parc Cenedlaethol Eryri in Welsh – was designated as a National Park in 1951, and lies in the north-west corner of Wales. It contains some of the most spectacular and tightly-packed mountain scenery in the United Kingdom.

It is a land of heather moors, lakes, wooded valleys, rivers, waterfalls, and brooding, craggy, mountain ranges, and a coastline with great sweeping bays.

Sheep farming, mining for minerals and slate quarrying have all left their marks on the landscape during the last few centuries. Some slate quarrying still exists, albeit on a smaller scale, and although many of the relics from mining and quarrying still remain, nature is steadily reclaiming the ruins which are still a fascinating feature of many parts of Snowdonia.

Each season in Snowdonia has its own beauty, from the colourful display of wild flowers in the Conwy Valley during springtime; the purple-clad heather moors above Bala in high summer; the golden autumnal colours of the ancient woods around Dolgellau; to the vast Arctic-like winter plateau of the Carneddau, the rugged Glyderau and especially majestic Snowdon (Yr Wyddfa), the highest summit in England and Wales.

Jerry Rawson

The cascades of Rhaeadr-fawr –
usually known as Aber Falls –
on the northern slopes of
the Carneddau near
Abergwyngregyn.

Opposite page:
The first light of a cold winter's
dawn adds a rosy-pink
hue to the Snowdon hills.

Storms sweep across Llyn Eigiau, situated in the
remote eastern section of the Carneddau.

A passing snow shower dusts the summit of
Pen Llithrig y Wrach in the eastern Carneddau.

The Afon Llugwy, swollen
by overnight rain, flows
through Capel Curig before
passing under a bridge where
it plunges over the Cyfyng Falls.

Opposite page:
Storm clouds sweep across
Snowdonia. The dramatic light
gives the scene atmosphere
and mood.

Autumn leaves are highlighted as the
Afon Llugwy flows silkily around a mossy boulder.

Opposite page:
An early morning view of Y Garn and Foel-goch
reflected in the calm waters of Llyn Ogwen.

Crags ring the top of Tryfan's north summit.

Opposite page:
Vibrant purple heather adds colour to this summer scene
of a stream rushing down the slopes from Llyn Idwal.

Cwm Idwal is redolent with
the history of Welsh rock climbing
Here, a climber balances his way
up Suicide Wall on the East Wall
of Cwm Idwal, with Llyn Idwal
in the background.

Opposite page:
The lingering light of a
summer evening picks out
the summit slopes of Pen yr Ole
Wen, reflected in Llyn Idwal.

Tryfan reflected in the waters of a tiny lake, often dry in summer,
situated below the craggy east face of Glyder Fach.

A scrambler in an exposed position on the spectacular pinnacled ridge of Cneifion Arete in Cwm Cneifion – often known as the Nameless Cwm – tucked above Cwm Idwal.

A sunlit boulder reflects the shape of Tryfan,
backed by the Carneddau, in this view
from the upper slopes of Glyder Fach.

Opposite page:
Gylder Fach reflected in Llyn y Caseg-fraith. The
pinnacled Bristly Ridge is visible on the right skyline.

Erosion by wind and rain has created this remarkable
cluster of rocks on the summit slopes of Glyder Fawr.

Opposite page:
The rocks at the top of Y Gribin, a ridge on Glyder Fach, lead the eye
across Llyn Idwal to Y Garn backed by Foel-goch, with the trench of
Nant Ffrancon, a classic glacial trough, on the right.

Fangs of rock covered in
rime ice, near the
summit of Glyder Fawr.

A misty autumn morning
by Llyn Padarn.

A summer's evening by Llyn Padarn near Llanberis, with the Snowdon range mirrored in the calm water.

The Snowdon hills in their winter blanket reflected in Llynnau Mymbyr,
near Capel Curig. A classic view of Snowdon.

Veils of mist swirl around the summits
of Snowdon (Yr Wyddfa) and Crib Goch.

Opposite page:
The sun sets beyond the Snowdon hills in this view
across Llynnau Mymbyr, near Capel Curig.

A solitary tree acts as a focal point in this winter
view across Nant Gwynant to Crib Goch.

Opposite page:
The Afon Glaslyn tumbles down the hillside below the mist-shrouded
Cwm Dyli on the eastern flanks of Snowdon (Yr Wyddfa).

Transparent ice coats stream-side grasses.

Opposite page:
The last rays of evening sunshine catch the summit slopes
of Moel Hebog in this view across Llyn Gwynant.

A vibrant mix of early
autumn colours add charm to
this view of the deep narrow gorge
of the Pass of Aberglaslyn,
near Beddgelert.

Opposite page:
Two fishermens' boats beside
Llyn y Dywarchen near Rhyd-Ddu.
Snowdon and its western
cwms dominate the
skyline ahead.

The Nantlle Ridge, one of the finest ridges in
Snowdonia, sweeps south-west from Y Garn.

The craggy buttresses on the northern flanks of Craig Cwm Silyn on the Nantlle Ridge, seen here across Llynnau Cwm Silyn.

Relics of slate quarrying in Cwm Orthin, seen across Llyn Cwmorthin, above Tanygrisiau, just west of Blaenau Ffestiniog.

Oppositte page:
The decaying ruins slowly being reclaimed by nature
are a reminder of the slate-quarrying days in Cwm Orthin.

A farmstead in Cwm Croesor backed by the Nantlle hills.

Opposite page:
Slate fences line up like tombstones at the disused Rhosydd slate quarry, on the high pass between Blaenau Ffestiniog and Croeser.

Pistyll Rhaerdr – one of the traditional wonders of Wales – in the Berwyn hills, to the north-east of Llangynog.

Opposite page:
Croesor, a village forever associated with the slate industry, which has formed such an integral part of the history and heritage of this region. The hill in the background is Moel Hebog.

Low evening sunlight casts long shadows across
the hillside near Llangynog, the Berwyn hills.

A patchwork of autumn
colours reflected in the
calm waters of
Llyn Tegid near Bala.

The fast flowing Afon Clywedog near
Dolgellau, on a damp autumn day.

Opposite page:
Misty morning on Llyn Tegid
looking south to Aran Benllyn.

The shapely hill of Carreg-y-saeth seen across Llyn Cwm Bycan, situated in the heart of the Rhinog range to the east of Harlech.

Opposite page:
Rhinog Fawr dominates the head of Cwm Nantcol.

A ruined farmhouse in Cwm Nantcol backed
by Rhinog Fawr and Rhinog Fach.

Dyffryn burial chamber, a
Neolithic site dating back to
3-4000 BC, in the
village of Dyffryn Ardudwy.

The superb sandy beach at Harlech.

The sand dunes at Harlech lead the eye towards Porthmadog, backed by the shapely peak of Moel Hebog.

The trees enliven this view across the slopes
of Craig Llwyd overlooking Minffordd.

Opposite page:
The last rays of the setting sun touch boulders and add warmth
to this view north across Tremadog Bay, from
the beach near Llandanwg.

A bird's-eye-view of Llyn Cau
from the summit slopes of
Pen y Gadair, the high point
of the Cadair Idris massif.

Opposite page:
An isolated farm at the foot
of Cwm Amarch overlooking
Llyn Mwyngil at Tal y Llyn.

The pointed peak of Pared y Cefn-hir overlooking Llyn Cregennen and its boat house.

Opposite page:
Two types of heather, ling and bell, and the golden flowers of gorse create a colourful foreground of this view above Llyn Cregennen near Arthog, with the Cadair Idris range in the background.

Sunrise across Llyn Cregennen
backed by the Cadair Idris range.

Evening light on the northern section of the
Cadair Idris range reflected in Llyn Cregennen.